THE UNOFFICIAL GUIDE TO
LEADERSHIP IN MINECRAFT®

JILL KEPPELER

PowerKiDS press

Published in 2026 by The Rosen Publishing Group, Inc.
2544 Clinton Street, Buffalo, NY 14224

Copyright © 2026 by The Rosen Publishing Group, Inc.

All rights reserved. No part of this book may be reproduced in any form without permission in writing from the publisher, except by a reviewer.

First Edition

Editor: Greg Roza
Book Design: Rachel Rising
Illustrator: Matías Lapegüe

Photo Credits: Cover, p. 1 Soloma/Shutterstock.com; Cover, p. 1, 3–24 SkillUp/Shutterstock.com; Cover, pp. 1, 3, 4, 7, 9, 10, 13, 15, 16, 19, 22–24 gersamina donnichi/Shutterstock.com; Cover, pp. 1, 3, 4, 7, 9, 10, 13, 15, 16, 19, 22–24 Oksana Kalashnykova/Shutterstock.com; p. 5 LightField Studios/Shutterstock.com.

Cataloging-in-Publication Data

Names: Keppeler, Jill.
Title: The unofficial guide to leadership in Minecraft / Jill Keppeler.
Description: Buffalo, New York : PowerKids Press, 2026. | Series: The unofficial guide to Minecraft social skills | Includes glossary and index.
Identifiers: ISBN 9781499452907 (pbk.) | ISBN 9781499452914 (library bound) | ISBN 9781499452921 (ebook)
Subjects: LCSH: Leadership in children–Juvenile literature. | Leadership–Juvenile literature. | Minecraft (Game)–Juvenile literature.
Classification: LCC BF723.L4 K47 2026 | DDC 158'.4-dc23

Manufactured in the United States of America

Minecraft is a trademark of Mojang (a game development studio owned by Microsoft Technology Corporation), and its use in this book does not imply a recommendation or endorsement of this title by Mojang or Microsoft.

Some of the images in this book illustrate individuals who are models. The depictions do not imply actual situations or events.

CPSIA Compliance Information: Batch #CSPK26. For Further Information contact Rosen Publishing at 1-800-237-9932.

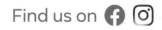

CONTENTS

STEPPING UP	4
FINDING DIRECTION	6
LEADERSHIP TRAITS	8
BECOMING A LEADER	12
SELF-CONFIDENCE	14
EMPATHY	16
NOT-SO-GREAT LEADERS	18
LEAD ON!	20
GLOSSARY	22
FOR MORE INFORMATION	23
INDEX	24

STEPPING UP

It can be fun to play video games like *Minecraft* by yourself. But it can be even more fun to play them with other people! But when there are more people in a *Minecraft* world, there can be more trouble. People can disagree, and disagreements can lead to problems. If these aren't resolved, or fixed, the problems can mess up all your fun.

Someone may need to step up and be a leader. Leaders can help a group make goals, set rules, and help people feel included. They can make the difference between a group that falls apart with arguing and a group that pulls together.

MINECRAFT MANIA

A *Minecraft* Realm is a **server** on which you can play with your friends. One of those friends (or likely a parent or another adult) will be the owner. They will need to invite people to play.

FINDING DIRECTION

When you're in a situation—whether in the real world or in *Minecraft*—and no one seems quite sure what to do, that's a time when you need a leader. Without one, everyone might just go their own way. This can be fine, but it might not be the best for many players. What if some people just want to build big, fancy cities and other people want to have an all-out battle and blow things up? That can't end well!

A leader will be the one who steps up and says, "OK, what can we agree on? What do we want? How can we make it happen?"

MINECRAFT MANIA

People have built some amazing things in *Minecraft*! This includes real working computers and scale copies of historic buildings such as the Sydney Opera House.

Sometimes cities (in history and in *Minecraft*) have big stone walls to protect them! They can be a useful addition to your city build.

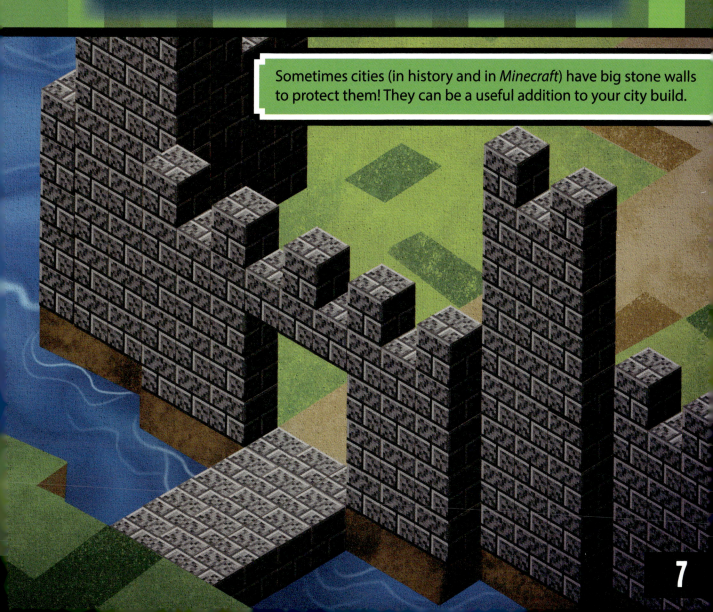

LEADERSHIP TRAITS

There are many kinds of leaders, but there are some traits, or qualities, that good ones have in common. Leaders will likely be good at seeing things from others' point of view, and they set an example for those they lead. They have good **communication** skills, and they speak up for their team members. When they make mistakes (everyone does!), they admit them.

Good leaders also value **diversity** in their group. They know everyone has different skills, and they know how to make everyone feel included. Many good leaders can help motivate a team, or give them a reason to act.

MINECRAFT MANIA

If you have a team goal of creating a large trading village in *Minecraft*, a good leader might start things by finding out what sort of setting the group wants for this village. Then, they'll organize people to start searching for that setting.

Minecraft villages are different depending on which **biome** they're in. Plains villages are the most common. Just as in the real world, plains biomes are mostly flat grasslands.

Another good leadership trait is knowing when to ask for help. No one is good at everything! This fits with knowing how to **delegate** jobs. What if someone in your group is great at fighting monsters, while another person creates amazing designs, or plans, for buildings? A good leader will know or learn this and ask the first person to protect the village area. They'll ask the second to work on new buildings.

Of course, good leaders do more than just ask other people to work. They'll be working right along with everyone else! Knowing what you're good at is just as important as knowing what others' skills are.

MINECRAFT MANIA

A group that decides to create a big trading village in *Minecraft* will likely start with a village that already exists. Each village will have a different combination of villager types.

One of the best types of *Minecraft* villagers to trade with is a librarian. They might have **enchanted** books to trade!

BECOMING A LEADER

Some people seem to be born leaders. Others just seem to listen to them and respect them. But really, anyone can learn the skills and traits of a good leader! This may be more difficult, or hard, for some people than for others, but it's not out of anyone's reach.

For example, perhaps you're shy and don't really like to talk to people. There's nothing wrong with being shy! But you can push yourself a bit to get a little out of your comfort zone if you need to talk. Perhaps **challenge** yourself to ask questions if someone's telling you a story.

MINECRAFT MANIA

There are many ways that being a good communicator can help you if you're playing with others in *Minecraft*. For one thing, you'll need to talk about **resources** and how to find and share them.

A leader can be skilled at talking others into doing what they want. That's one reason why it's so important to have good leaders—and to know what good leaders are like!

SELF-CONFIDENCE

Self-confidence can be a big part of being a good leader. This means that you're sure of yourself and what you can do. People are more likely to follow those who seem like they know their own strengths. In a *Minecraft* world, you could see this as someone who knows the game well enough to figure out the different steps needed to reach the group's goals. Then they **assign** them (fairly) to the group members.

Being self-confident doesn't mean you brag all the time! It just means you know what to do and then do it. Leaders make mistakes too—but they also figure out how to fix their mistakes.

MINECRAFT MANIA

 When you're setting up a base in a *Minecraft* village, you'll need to light up the village to be sure monsters don't **spawn** in it. If you don't, you could lose all your villagers and be attacked too!

In some kinds of *Minecraft*, a village can have a zombie **siege**! This means many zombies spawn into a village no matter how well lit it is.

EMPATHY

Empathy is another trait that many good leaders have. This means they are aware of the feelings of others and feel what it would be like to be in their position. Some people think that some gaming, as in *Minecraft*, other video games, and board games, can help people be more empathetic! If you're playing a role, or part, that's different from your usual role, you can better understand how other people might feel.

A leader in a *Minecraft* game might see another player who's struggling to hold up their part and realize that they feel unhappy. Games are supposed to be fun! Maybe that player would feel better with different responsibilities.

MINECRAFT MANIA

Imagine you're playing *Minecraft* with a new group, and they say you have to build houses when what you really want to do is explore. A good leader will understand and help change things.

When people don't feel heard or understood, they often don't want to take part in things anymore. But when leaders have empathy and understanding, more people will want to play.

17

NOT-SO-GREAT LEADERS

Leadership is often a good thing, but sometimes, the people who step up as leaders aren't good leaders. They don't listen to others. They may have no empathy. They might just like telling others what to do. It's important to recognize that not every leader is someone you should follow.

So, what should you do after you realize this? In a setting like a *Minecraft* game, you can just say that, no, you won't follow that person. Once someone does this, more people will likely follow. In fact, part of being a good leader can be standing up to bad leaders!

MINECRAFT MANIA

One time when a good leader can come in handy in *Minecraft* is when a village raid is going on. During a raid, villagers and other mobs attack a village in waves. A good leader can help organize a **defense**.

Many kinds of mobs may take part in a village raid. One of the most dangerous is a ravager. These big beasts are much stronger than most players!

LEAD ON!

    Knowing the traits of a good leader can be helpful in many ways. You'll be better prepared to look for good leaders in friend groups and in school—and when gaming, including in *Minecraft* worlds. And when the time comes to be a leader yourself, you can step up.

    Remember that leaders aren't always the ones with swords at the front of a charge into battle against zombies and creepers. Sometimes they're the ones who make sure everyone in the group has enough resources and a good base. Sometimes they're both. What kind of leader do you think you'll be?

GLOSSARY

assign: To give someone a task or amount of work to do.

biome: A natural community of plants and animals, such as a forest or desert.

challenge: To give yourself or others something that is difficult, or hard, to do.

communication: The use of words, sounds, signs, or behaviors to convey ideas, thoughts, and feelings.

defense: The act of defending, or working to keep safe.

delegate: To give a job to another person.

diversity: The quality or state of having many different types, forms, or ideas.

enchanted: To be affected as if by magic. In Minecraft, an enchantment is a way of giving tools and weapons better or extra abilities.

resource: Something that can be used.

server: A computer in a network that provides services or files to others.

siege: A persistent, or ongoing, attack.

spawn: To first appear.

FOR MORE INFORMATION

BOOKS

Clarke, Adam, and Victoria Bennett. *Unofficial Minecraft Life Hacks Lab for Kids.* Beverly, MA: Quarry Books, 2019.

Mojang AB. *Minecraft: Guide to PVP Minigames.* New York, NY: Random House Worlds: 2018.

Sornson, Bob. *Stand in My Shoes: Kids Learning About Empathy.* Early Learning Foundation, 2021.

WEBSITES

Discover Which Historical Ruler You're Like
kids.nationalgeographic.com/games/personality-quizzes/article/discover-which-historical-ruler-youre-like
Learn more about historical leaders with this quiz from National Geographic Kids.

Raid
minecraft.wiki/w/Raid
Learn more about pillager raids on the Minecraft Wiki.

Publisher's note to educators and parents: Our editors have carefully reviewed these websites to ensure that they are suitable for students. Many websites change frequently, however, and we cannot guarantee that a site's future contents will continue to meet our high standards of quality and educational value. Be advised that students should be closely supervised whenever they access the internet.

INDEX

C

communication, 8, 13

D

delegate, 10
diversity, 8

E

empathy, 16, 17, 18

G

goals, 4, 9, 14

L

leadership traits, 8, 10, 12, 16, 20
listen, 12, 18

M

mistakes, 8, 14
motivate, 8

O

organize, 9, 19

R

respect, 12

S

self-confidence, 14